Fact Finders

THE
INVENTION
OF THE
COMPUTER

Lucy Beevor

Raintree is an imprint of Capstone Global Library Limited, a company incorporated in England and Wales
having its registered office at 264 Banbury Road, Oxford, OX2 7DY – Registered company number: 66955

www.raintree.co.uk
myorders@raintree.co.uk

Edited by Jennifer Huston
Designed by Heidi Thompson
Original illustrations © Capstone Global Library Ltd 2018
Picture research by Eric Gohl
Production by Katy LaVigne
Originated by Capstone Global Library Ltd
Printed and bound in Inida.

Original Edition Author
Gayle Worland

ISBN 978 1 4747 5283 1 (hardback)
22 21 20 19 18
10 9 8 7 6 5 4 3 2 1

ISBN 978 1 4747 5295 4 (paperback)
22 21 20 19 18
10 9 8 7 6 5 4 3 2 1

British Library Cataloguing in Publication Data
A full catalogue record for this book is available from the British Library.

Acknowledgements
We would like to thank the following for permission to reproduce photographs:
Alamy: B Christopher, 17, Szasz-Fabian Jozsef, 14; Getty Images: Bletchley Park Trust, 13, Historical, 11, Justin Sullivan, 18,
Science & Society Picture Library, 9 (top); iStockphoto: bowdenimages, 24, iEverest, 19; Library of Congress: 8; Newscom:
akg-images, 6, 10, Heritage Images/Ann Ronan Picture Library, 9 (bottom), SOLO Syndication/Les Wilson, 12, Xinhua News
Agency/Yao Qilin, 4, YNA/Yonhap News, 5, ZUMA Press/Michael Quan, 20; Shutterstock: Andrei Kuzmik, 15, Artsplav,
cover (bottom right), BARS graphics, 28 (top left), GOLFX, 7, ifong, cover (top middle), 23, Igor Klimov, cover (top right), 28
(middle), LeoSad, 16, lumen-digital, 27, Mr.Creative, 28 (top right), notbad, 28 (bottom middle), oknoart, cover (bottom left),
PanicAttack, cover (top left), Pixel 4 Images, 21, PureSolution, 2–3, Rawpixel.com, 25, sakkmesterke, 26, Scanrail1, cover
(middle right), T. Lesia, 1, Wiktoria Matynia, 28 (bottom right)
Design Elements: Shutterstock

CONTENTS

MAN VERSUS MACHINE

In March 2016, people around the world tuned in to watch as a man played a video game called Go. The man was the world's top Go player, Lee Sedol from South Korea. He was playing against a computer program called AlphaGo.

Go is an ancient Chinese board game for two players. The aim is to use your stones to surround more territory than your opponent. Both players and programmers thought it would be years before a computer could win a game of Go against a human.

A large crowd gathered to watch the world's top Go player, Lee Sedol, take on a computer program.

Sedol makes a move during a game of Go against a computer program called AlphaGo.

That all changed when Sedol faced AlphaGo in a five-game match. AlphaGo won the first three games. Sedol won the fourth, but he had already lost overall. AlphaGo also won the fifth and final game. The program had beaten one of the best Go players of all time.

For many people, it showed that computers could be smarter than people. Others said to remember that people make computers.

BEFORE COMPUTERS

People have always looked for ways to make their work easier. Before computers were invented, people built tools and machines to help them solve mathematical problems.

Blaise Pascal (1623–1662)

PASCAL'S CALCULATOR

Blaise Pascal was a French **mathematician** and inventor whose father worked as a tax collector. Pascal wanted to make a machine that would help his father **calculate** tax sums. In 1642 he invented a mechanical calculator. It used gears and levers to add and subtract numbers.

THE ABACUS

The **abacus** was the first tool that helped people add and subtract. It was invented in Asia thousands of years ago. The abacus had beads on rods inside a wooden frame. People used it to add and subtract by moving the beads up and down the rods.

People used the abacus to add and subtract numbers.

mathematician expert in mathematics
calculate find a solution by using maths
abacus ancient machine used to add and subtract

INVENTORS

The modern computer wasn't invented overnight. Many years of research and tests went into making the modern computer.

CHARLES BABBAGE

In the early 1820s, English inventor Charles Babbage began working on a calculator that could also print out results in a table. He called his machine the Difference Engine. Babbage never finished building the Difference Engine, but if he had, it would have been the first automatic calculating device.

In 1832, Babbage began designing a new machine called the Analytical Engine. He wanted it to calculate maths problems and remember them.

Charles Babbage's Analytical Engine was going to be powered by steam.

THE FIRST COMPUTER PROGRAMMER

In 1842, English mathematician Ada Lovelace added notes to a paper about the Analytical Engine. The notes included the first **algorithm** used to calculate sums. Many call this the first computer program. Lovelace was the first person to see that computers could be used for tasks other than maths. She predicted that computers would become a huge part of our lives.

Ada Lovelace (1815–1852) was the daughter of the famous poet Lord Byron.

Babbage tried hard to build his machine, but he couldn't get all of its gears and wheels to fit together. Babbage never finished the Analytical Engine but, more than 100 years later, other inventors used his ideas.

A section of Babbage's Difference Engine is shown here. If the entire thing had been built, it would have been nearly 2.4 metres (8 feet) tall and weighed almost 4 tonnes (4 tons).

algorithm step-by-step procedure for solving a problem, especially by a computer

HOWARD H. AIKEN

In 1944, Howard H. Aiken built the first electronic calculator, which he nicknamed the Harvard Mark I. Aiken's Mark I was based on Babbage's Difference and Analytical Engines. It was more than 15 metres (50 feet) long and used 805 kilometres (500 miles) of wires.

The Mark I calculator is on display at Harvard University in Boston, Massachusetts, USA.

ECKERT AND MAUCHLY

In 1946, John Presper Eckert and John W. Mauchly created the first programmable electronic computer at the University of Pennsylvania. They called it the ENIAC, which stands for Electronic Numerical Integrator and Computer.

ENIAC was as large as two small houses and weighed 27 tonnes (30 tons). It could calculate numbers a thousand times faster than a person using an abacus. It could also solve 5,000 addition problems and 360 to 500 multiplication tasks per second.

Many people helped run the ENIAC. They did so by flipping switches and plugging in or unplugging wires.

DID YOU KNOW?

Although it could quickly solve mathematical problems, the ENIAC used a lot of electricity. Whenever the computer was being used, the lights around the university dimmed.

ALAN TURING

During World War II (1939–1945), the **Allies** were at war with the **Axis powers**. The Axis powers communicated in codes to keep their battle plans secret. They used a machine called Enigma to send their coded messages.

During the war, the Allies worked at the Government Code and Cypher School at Bletchley Park, trying to crack the codes. In 1939, Alan Turing invented a machine called the Bombe, which cracked the Enigma's codes. By the end of the war, more than 200 Bombes were in use. Turing's invention of the Bombe was a major factor in helping the Allies win the war.

From 1945 to 1947, Turing designed the ACE (Automatic Computing Engine). It was the first computer to store computer programs inside the machine. Many modern computers are based on the ACE.

Alan Turing's "Bombe" helped the Allies to crack 3,000 enemy messages per day.

Allies group of countries, including Britain, France and the United States, that fought together in World War II

Axis powers group of countries, including Germany, Italy and Japan, that fought together in World War II

TOMMY FLOWERS

In 1941, Tommy Flowers began working with Turing on the Enigma codes. He was asked to design an automatic **decoder**. This would help save time because the decoder could crack the codes faster than a person. By December 1943, Flowers had designed and built the Colossus Mark I. It was an excellent code breaker, but it was also the world's first programmable electronic computer.

Within a year, Flowers had built the Colossus Mark II, which was even more powerful than the Mark I. It was immediately used to crack important German codes. This valuable information helped the Allies to plan a successful invasion of German-occupied France, known as D-Day, on 6 June 1944. The Allies' success on D-Day eventually led to their victory in the war in 1945.

By the end of the war, 10 Colossus Mark II devices were being used to break coded German messages.

decoder person or machine that cracks codes

THE COMPUTER CHANGES

After the mid-1900s, people began building smaller computers that worked faster than the ENIAC. These computers could also do more than solve mathematical problems.

THE VACUUM TUBE

Early computers used glass containers called vacuum tubes that controlled electric signals. But vacuum tubes needed a lot of electricity. They also got very hot and broke easily. Computers needed a better way to control the signals.

Vacuum tubes were used in all types of electronics, including radios, televisions and recording equipment.

THE TRANSISTOR

In 1947, scientists at the Bell Laboratories in New Jersey, USA, invented the transistor. A transistor did the same job as a vacuum tube, but it was much smaller, cheaper and stronger. The transistor meant that computers could be made much smaller and lighter. This invention changed computers forever.

A transistor was much smaller than a vacuum tube. In fact, it was smaller than a penny.

THE MICROCHIP

After the invention of the transistor, computers changed even more. In the 1950s, several scientists worked together to develop the computer "chip", which could store a lot of information in a very small space. American engineer Jack Kilby was the first to demonstrate a working chip on 12 September 1958.

By 1971, computer chips had become even smaller. At that time, scientists discovered how to put most of a computer's calculating parts on a chip smaller than a fingernail. Thousands of transistors could fit onto this **microchip** called a microprocessor.

Microchips are smaller than a fingernail.

As the transistor and microchip got smaller, so did computers. Over time, computers could sit on top of desks instead of filling large rooms.

microchip tiny circuit that processes information in a computer

THE FIRST PERSONAL COMPUTER

The first computers to use microprocessors appeared in the early 1970s. Many of these computers came as kits. One of these early kit computers was the Altair 8800, which was invented in 1974. Thousands of individuals and businesses bought the Altair 8800 kit. The Altair 8800 had lights on the front, and owners could write computer programs to make the lights blink.

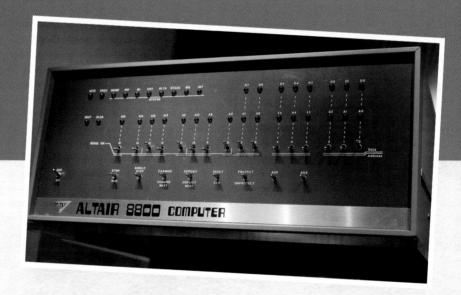

MICROSOFT

In 1975, computer programmers Bill Gates and Paul Allen began working with the Altair 8800's inventors. Gates and Allen had invented a program that could **interpret** a collection of computer languages called BASIC. They called their company Micro-soft. A year later, they changed the name to Microsoft. The company soon began making personal computers (PCs) that anyone could buy and use in their home. Microsoft went on to become the world's largest PC and **software** company.

Bill Gates co-founded Microsoft, the most successful PC company in history.

interpret explain in a different language
software programs used by a computer

APPLE COMPUTER, INC.

In the late 1970s, Steve Jobs and Stephen Wozniak started Apple Computer, Inc. In 1984, Apple created the Macintosh (Mac) computer. It had more functions than the Altair 8800, including a control called a mouse to open programs. The Mac's screen also had icons, or pictures, that allowed people to use the computer without typing in codes. Like Microsoft, Apple has changed computers forever.

Apple's Macintosh computers from the mid-1980s had a screen, a keyboard and a mouse.

Companies such as Microsoft and Apple made it possible for almost anyone to own a computer. But another invention was about to change the world again.

THE WORLD WIDE WEB

Tim Berners-Lee worked for the European Organization for Nuclear Research known as CERN. In 1980, he created a database to help CERN scientists share information. Berners-Lee wrote the information using **hypertext** and **hyperlinks**. This was the first website.

By 1989, Berners-Lee had connected the first website to others and given the websites domain names, or web addresses. With that, the World Wide Web was born!

British computer scientist Tim Berners-Lee

hypertext text on a web page that contains links to other text
hyperlink piece of text on a web page that is linked to another web page, so that when you click on it, you go to the second web page

EMAIL ARRIVES

The first form of email was invented in 1965. Messages were stored on a central disc and accessed from different computers on the same network, usually within universities or the military. But with the invention of the World Wide Web in 1989, programmers were finally able to create email systems that could send messages online. In 1993, AOL and Microsoft Outlook invented the first modern email servers. This opened up email to everyone, and it quickly became popular. Today, email is one of the most common forms of communication.

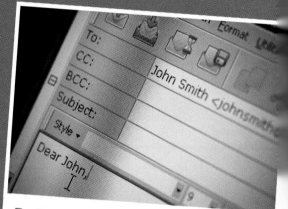

By the mid-1990s, email was available to anyone with a computer and an Internet connection.

As its name implies, the World Wide Web quickly spread around the world. Now there are websites for everything from cooking to cat videos. The World Wide Web allows people to use email and social media, and to quickly search for and find information. It connects people, businesses and organizations globally.

HOW COMPUTERS WORK

Numbers make computers work. Computers understand only two numbers – 0 and 1 – which are called **binary digits**. These numbers tell the computer what to do. A 0 turns off an electric signal. A 1 turns on an electric signal. Every letter, number and picture on a computer has its own set of 0s and 1s.

DECIMAL NUMBER	BINARY DIGIT
0	0
1	1
2	10
3	11
4	100
5	101
6	110
7	111
8	1000
9	1001
10	1010

Each decimal number has its own combination of binary digits.

THE PARTS OF A COMPUTER

Computers are made up of hardware and software. The hardware is the machine and the parts that make it work. The software is made up of the programs a computer uses.

Today, computers come in different sizes. Desktop computers have a monitor like a TV screen. Some have a tower. All of the calculations happen in the tower. In some desktops the tower is inside the monitor. The keyboard and mouse allow you to tell the computer what to do.

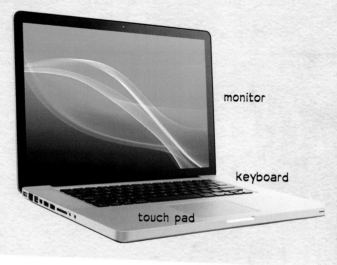

monitor

keyboard

touch pad

Laptops are small, light and easy to carry around.

With a laptop, the hardware, software and the screen or monitor are all in one. The keyboard and touch pad are also part of the laptop.

binary digit either of two numbers, usually 0 and 1

2

COMPUTERS TODAY

Today, computers are faster and can store more information than ever before. And they can be used nearly anywhere. Most people own a computer or laptop, and almost everyone uses some type of computer at school or work.

Computers are used in many different types of businesses, including supermarkets.

Supermarket staff use computers to scan items and calculate totals when you pay at the checkout. Mechanics use computers to test cars and find out what is wrong with them.

Millions of people also use computers for learning. Many libraries and schools have computers. The computers help adults and children to find information on the Internet. Students use computers to research and write reports.

Computers are used for fun activities too. People use them to play video games and watch films. Computers are also used to create TV programmes, cartoons and adverts.

Computers are often used to teach or research information.

INTERNET SAFETY

Some people use computers to commit crimes. Computer viruses can stop other computers from working. Criminals can use computers to steal private information, films or computer games.

The Internet has made it easier to share information, but sometimes this information can get into the wrong hands. It is important to be safe when using the Internet. Never give out your personal information to anyone you don't know. This includes your name, your telephone number, and your home and email address.

Internet safety is very important. Always ask an adult to help you when you're searching on the Internet.

EVEN SMALLER COMPUTERS

Over time, computers have become smaller and smaller. **Tablets**, **smartphones** and even some watches use computers. Many also have touch screens, which allow the user to tell the computer what to do by touching the icons on the screen. People carry tablets and smartphones with them to use outside the home.

Computers have changed people's lives. They make work easier. Computers help people to find information and solve problems faster. They are essential tools for the modern world.

Today's computers come in many different sizes.

tablet small, portable computer that you can use by touching the screen with your fingers or by typing on a keyboard
smartphone mobile phone that allows the user to access the Internet and send and receive emails, as well as run programs and applications

2

HOW WE USE COMPUTERS

Here are some of the most common home computer activities today:

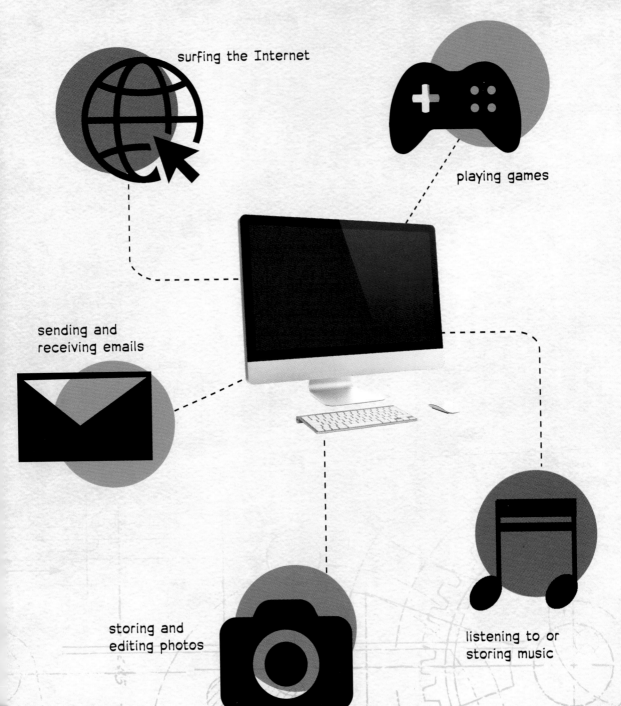

surfing the Internet

playing games

sending and
receiving emails

storing and
editing photos

listening to or
storing music

TIMELINE ------------------------------------

1642	Blaise Pascal invents the first mechanical calculator
1832	Charles Babbage begins designing, but never builds, the Analytical Engine
1842	Ada Lovelace writes the first algorithm to calculate sums
1939	Alan Turing invents a machine called the Bombe to crack enemy codes during World War II
1943	Tommy Flowers designs and builds the Colossus Mark I to crack enemy codes; it is the world's first programmable computer
1944	Howard H. Aiken builds the first electronic calculator; that same year, Tommy Flowers builds the Colossus Mark II, which immediately provides vital information to help the Allies during the D-Day invasion
1946	John Presper Eckert and John W. Mauchly finish building the first programmable electronic computer, the ENIAC
1947	Alan Turing finishes his design for the ACE (Automatic Computing Engine), the first computer to store computer programs inside the machine; that same year, scientists at the Bell Laboratories in New Jersey, USA, invent the transistor
1958	American engineer Jack Kilby demonstrates the first working computer "chip" to the US Air Force
1965	The first electronic messages (email) are sent at the Massachusetts Institute of Technology (MIT), in the United States
1971	Scientists invent the microprocessor (microchip)
1974	The Altair 8800 is invented
1975	Bill Gates and Paul Allen start Micro-soft, now called Microsoft
1984	Apple Computer, Inc., launches the Macintosh (Mac) computer
1989	Tim Berners-Lee invents the World Wide Web
1993	AOL and Microsoft Outlook launch the first modern email systems
2016	Computer program AlphaGo beats the world's top Go player, Lee Sedol of South Korea

GLOSSARY

abacus ancient machine used to add and subtract

algorithm step-by-step procedure for solving a problem, especially by a computer

Allies group of countries, including Britain, France and the United States, that fought together in World War II

Axis powers group of countries including Germany, Italy and Japan that fought together in World War II

binary digit either of two numbers, usually 0 and 1

calculate find a solution by using mathematics

decoder person or machine that cracks codes

hyperlink piece of text on a web page that is linked to another web page, so that when you click on it, you go to the second web page

hypertext text on a web page that contains links to other text

interpret explain in a different language

mathematician expert in mathematics

microchip tiny circuit that processes information in a computer

smartphone mobile phone that allows users to access the Internet and send and receive emails, as well as run programs and applications

software programs used by a computer

tablet small, portable computer that you can use by touching the screen with your fingers or by typing on a keyboard

COMPREHENSION QUESTIONS

1. Before the computer was invented, people used the abacus, and later the calculator, to help them with maths problems. They went to libraries to get information from books. In what ways have computers made learning easier today?

2. Choose two computers from the book, one early and one modern. Using the text and photos, compare and contrast the two computers. How has the modern computer changed from the early one?

3. Today, many people have smartphones that are like minicomputers. Think about how people use smartphones like computers. What are the good things about having a minicomputer in a smartphone? What are the bad things?

FIND OUT MORE

Ada Lovelace, Poet of Science: The First Computer Programmer, Diane Stanley (Simon & Schuster/Paula Wiseman Books, 2016)

Spies and Codebreakers (Heroes of World War II), ClaireThrop (Raintree, 2015)

Tim Berners-Lee (Inspirational Lives), Claudia Martin (Wayland Publishers, 2017)

Today's Technology (Infographic How it Works), Jon Richards, ed. (Wayland Publishers, 2016)

WEBSITES

www.bbc.co.uk/guides/ztrq7ty
Discover more about how computers have changed over time.

kids.britannica.com/students/article computer/273764#199040.toc
This in-depth article offers an overview of the history of computers.

www.dkfindout.com/uk/computer-coding/what-is-internet/
Learn more about how the Internet works.

INDEX